# Disclaimer & Copyright

I0101685

## Disclaimer

This book has been written for guidance only. It should be used as a potential idea of how you can achieve your end goal of writing a fiction novel.

Excalibur Press are under no circumstances claiming this is the only way to write a fiction novel. We also acknowledge that this method may not work for everyone.

Following the instructions in this guide will not guarantee that your book will be accepted by a publisher.

## Copyright

This edition published in 2016
by Excalibur Press


ISBN: 978-0-9935015-7-9

Formatting & layout by
Excalibur Press

Excalibur Press
Belfast, Northern Ireland

team@excaliburpress.co.uk
@ExcaliburPress
www.excaliburpress.co.uk

# Introduction

How many times have you heard the expression "I'm writing a book"? And how many times have you replied "So am I"?

The reality is most people WANT to write a novel and have even put pen to paper - so to speak - but the question is "are they actually writing a book?"

We've all been there. We've spent hours imagining the characters, scenes, plot-lines and much more. For many of us we've even started writing, aimlessly typing as the words pour out.

Eventually things come to a standstill, we're not quite sure if what we've written even works and usually, at some point, we arrive at a point of the narrative that we haven't quite crafted in our heads, and for some reason it isn't flowing like the rest.

Probably the worst thing we do is beat ourselves up for not being able to pump out book after book like all those other writers we've heard of who make it big with their first novel and now they're writing several every year.

Let's get a little reality check here...have a "wise up" moment with me...

Most writers, like many creative people, spent a long time on their first work - for some they spent years pulling together their creative piece of writing, music or art. All the while we've got lives, jobs, kids, homes, illness, family life, social life, relationships and much more to juggle.

Those 40 hours a week we put in to pay the bills...that's when these writers are writing, so it's no wonder they're knocking out several books a year. Give yourself a

break.

The very fact that you've got it to this point means you want to get to that finish line and hopefully we can help you with this Quick & Easy Guide To Finishing Your Fiction Novel.

The biggest thing you need to consider when reading and implementing some of the steps in this book is to realise that it is not the only way to write a fiction novel.  In fact, you might find that it doesn't work for you - that's ok.  What it may do, in that case, is help you develop your own formula.

What we want to achieve from this guide is to help you go from that person who has been writing a book their whole lives to be well on your way to becoming a published author.

If you want to know more about how you can take the step from bedroom writer to published author don't be afraid to get in touch with us at Excalibur Press where we can help you Unleash The Power Of Your Words.  It's less expensive than you think to DIY!

*"We believe every book deserves a space on the shelf"*

**- Excalibur Press -**

Knowing exactly what you're writing about can often help to wade through the thoughts all whizzing around in your head.

You know you have a good story, you're maybe even confident about your plot and characters...but getting it all in one place where you can show someone else or simply take a look with a fresh eye yourself can be more beneficial than you think.

## Here are 6 things we recommend you do:

### 1. Book Description

In no more than 200 words DESCRIBE YOUR BOOK, condensing your story on paper will actually help to you to develop it. This will also give you something to always refer to in order to make sure you're staying true to our original idea.

### 2. Define Your Book

Identify what GENRE you are writing in, or if it's across more than one genre write them down. It might be a good idea to note some writing styles that work in the genre(s) that you are writing in, it's good to give fans a little taste of what they know with your unique take.

*TOP TIP: You could even put some examples of similar books in these genres to help you focus on what your reader will want. We would recommend also putting the cover art down as well - to give you an idea of what your audience will respond to.*

# Part 1 - About Your Book

### 3. Visual Stimulation

In no more than 200 words write a MOVIE TRAILER for your book.

We know this sounds a little off-the-wall, but if you can imagine the "movie trailer guy" describe your book it will also help create some visual stimulations for you and your book.

You might find you may even see things that you hadn't thought of before.

Try watching a few on YouTube, especially in the same genre of your book, it will help you get "in the zone".

### 4. Spoil It

In no more than 200 words write a SPOILER for your book.  This is basically the same as the movie trailer but you have to give the whole game away.

It will also come in very handy when you get stuck, condensing your spoiler into 200 words or less will help you identify the key element of the plot line that you should then use as a guidance point for the rest of the book.

## 5. Who Are Your Readers?

Identify and write down who your TARGET AUDIENCE is.

Describe them, what else do they like?  What TV shows or films do they like?  What other authors do they read?  Is there a certain age group?

You will be surprised how handy this comes in at a later date.


## 6. Plot It Out

Now it's time to write that longer PLOT SYNOPSIS.  Keep it around 500-700 words and pretend that you are writing it to send to a potential publisher.  Your book description, movie trailer and spoiler will all help with this.

Each of these steps will all seem very repetitive but they will help you to focus on what is important with you book's plot and story, apart from that when you're finished all you need is a swift rewrite of them all and you're ready to go with your marketing plan.

*TOP TIP: Now is a good time to get some feedback.  Start with your movie trailer, if someone responds well you could let them read the spoiler or plot synopsis (make sure you check if they want to know the whole plot - if not the book description may be your best bet).*

*Don't be afraid to ask people for honest feedback and explain to them that you WANT to hear it whether it's good or bad.  And of course, we don't need to tell you - don't let it knock your confidence if they don't tell you what you are hoping to hear.*

# Part 2 - Breaking It Down

# Part 2 - Breaking It Down

Now you have a good basis from which to start planning the elements of your book.

Time to break it down and expand. You don't have to write a whole lot and it doesn't have to be in manuscript, it can be in note form, bullet points, brain-storm - whatever works for you.

## Here are 4 areas we recommend you expand:

### 1. Background

It's time to SET THE SCENE, here you can jot down or start writing things like - when is your book set, where, what season, what part of the city/country.

Another consideration here would be to think about the opening scene of the book and to begin jotting down ideas for the end scene.

### 2. Central Theme

Ask yourself what is the MAIN EVENT or main thread in the plot-line.

Start doing some basic writing of ideas and thoughts and brainstorming around this - don't worry if this is random ramblings or streams of consciousness.

By getting these down on paper you're opening the flood-gates to allow your brain to continue a creative flow without being blocked.

*TOP TIP: If you're going to note-take or use a scribble book, we recommend that you transfer it to digital within a few days. This can help you formulate and remind yourself of the ideas you were jotting down and, in some cases, eliminate the things that just won't fit.*

# Part 2 - Breaking It Down

### 3. Hook Them In

Identify your TWIST or HOOK, start thinking about the logistics of this, how will you integrate it into the story, how much will you reveal and when, who will be the key character involved, how central is it to the main story.

This sounds a bit obvious, but like many of the other steps it's asking you to think about just one aspect of the book, rather than the entire concept.

Again you may feel that random jottings and scribbles might help you release all that information your storing inside when you think about your book sub-consciously or when you're on the move.

Don't put yourself under pressure, you can always come back this, just make sure you identify the hook or twist that you want to build into your story, especially if it's going to be integral to the ending.

### 4. The End

One of the things that can really play on our mind is the ENDING of our book. And most of us probably won't really know how we want this to go down until we get right into the writing of the manuscript.

However, with this playing away in our sub-conscious and scenarios running round our brain we can more often than not end up thinking more about something we don't need to know yet than what we're actually working on.

# Part 2 - Breaking It Down

By doing some brainstorming, note taking and brain dumping on paper and allowing your stream of consciousness to play out you can effectively clear up some space for the bits you do need and want to concentrate on.

Many writers develop various endings to their books and finally settle on the one that fits best with their final development of the story.

Take into consideration things such as whether or not you want to develop a series of novels, remember to ensure you don't leave your ending too open... people must feel like they've come to a conclusion even if you're setting up for further mystery and revellations in book 2.

**TOP TIP:** If you find certain parts of the book keep creeping into your consciousness when you're doing something else - it's a good idea to write down everything you're thinking.

It's your brain's way of telling you that you need to take note. You may or may not find it useful in the future but it will help you spring clean your thought process.

*"We want to help you unleash the power of your words"*

**- Excalibur Press -**

# Part 3 - Meet Your Characters

You may think you know everything about every one of your characters, but the truth is, you maybe haven't fully formed each of them yet.

By getting to know your characters better you will be able to develop dialogue and behaviour patterns better throughout your manuscript.

This will also mean you have something to refer back to every time you get stuck with a character.

One thing that happens a lot in fiction writing is the need to change certain aspects of your character, even something as basic as the name, by keeping character sheets you can keep track of things like this much easier.

## Here is a handy table you can fill out for each character:

| Name of character | |
|---|---|
| Age | |
| Profession | |
| Location | |
| Describe their personality as if you're talking to a friend | |
| Describe their appearance as if you're talking to a friend | |
| Does your character have any specific quirks or traits? | |
| Character connections - such as are they related to or in a relationship with another character | |
| Who would play your character in a movie (this helps you to create a visual of your character in your mind while writing) | |

Every Accomplishment Starts With the Decision to *Try.*

# Part 4 - Break It Down...Even Further

Now for some real preparation. Time to give yourself some goals and a basis to start some structured writing.

We advise that free writing is incredibly important for most writers - ie, just sitting down and typing and typing and typing until you can't type anymore.

However, there will come a time when you need to begin structuring it all, and this step can help in pulling everything together.

We've found that for some writers swapping between brain storming on paper, free writing and structured planning can help release creative blocks and tension. By changing the medium and the delivery it's possible to think differently and ideas that maybe couldn't have developed in a brain storm or free writing might come out in a structured writing session and vice versa.

By breaking down your book writing into small bitesized chunks you will find that the finish line gets closer and the hill less steep.

## Here are 4 areas we recommend you look at in this stage:

### 1. Set Targets

It's time to set some TARGETS, for example, have you thought about the length you want to write to.

Maybe you prefer to start with a short story or a novella and then graduate to a full novel?

Whatever you want to do it's a good idea to have a target in place.

Don't forget it doesn't have to be strictly adhered to, it just has to give you something to work towards and you can amend it as you go along to suit your project.

# Part 4 - Break It Down...Even Further

## 2. Word Count?

How many CHAPTERS do you want to write? Now is a good time to decide this and give yourself a rough estimate of how many words you want per chapter, giving you a rough goal to work towards.

Don't set this in stone, it's merely a guideline to help you develop writing targets. Some people like to write in small burst of time, others choose a longer amount of time and attach a writing target.

There is no formula for how many words you should, could or can write - every writer is very different. So don't beat yourself up if it's taking time, let the words come naturally and don't worry about editing as you go along - certainly make some changes, but leave the real editing to the end (or the professionals).

## 3. Chapter Planning

Why not try some CHAPTER SYNOPSIS', by laying out each chapter and describing what it will contain in a few lines you will be able to begin to structure your story in such a way that it starts to become a case of simply filling in the blanks.

A chapter synopsis also helps you guage whether or not you're getting too bogged down with one part of the story and sometimes can help you consider whether something is more important than you first thought.

## 4. Further Planning

Now let's try to EXPAND THE CHAPTERS, by going back to your chapter synopsis' and expanding each of them with some more information you can start to see whether or not the flow of your story will work. Maybe this is the time to add more chapters or chop some out.

*TOP TIP: It's very easy to keep your writing to yourself, especially when it's not finished. But sometimes letting others read over your synopsis' or character development information they may see things you didn't. You're under no obligation to take people's advice or suggestions, however, their constructive criticism or keen eye could save you hours in the future.*

*"I always try to tell a good story, one with a compelling plot that will keep the pages turning. That is my first and primary goal"*

**- John Grisham -**

# Part 5 - When You Need A Break

Don't dream your life, live your dream

# Part 5 - When You Need A Break

No matter why you write, it's important to understand that EVERYONE encounters "creative block" or "writer's block" as many people call it.

However, this can be intensely frustrating when you don't want to walk away from your project because despite having a creative block you may be enthused about your book and have a lot of ideas and thought swimming around in your brain.

## Here are 8 things we recommend you do when the dreaded writer's block strikes and you don't want to stop working on your book:

### 1. On The Front

Maybe it's time to start thinking about your COVER, from working out how you are going to get it designed to what you want it to be.  It's a good idea to get a document put together of covers you like and a little information as to why you like them - that way you can just give it to whoever is doing your cover.

Before you contract your designer it's a good idea to check online sellers who specialise in creating professional and good quality covers.

However, it is important that if you're going to use a photograph that you check three things:

- Make sure you have permission to use the photograph you have selected for commercial purposes.  Even if it's a picture from a friend, ask for confirmation in writing.

- That the picture is of high enough quality in order to print clearly.  Whilst it may look good on your computer or tablet screen, it's essential to be sure it will print, especially if you're going to sell on Amazon or get a batch of your book printed.

- Don't over-crowd your cover with too much information.  Take your lead from the biggest authors in your category.

*TOP TIP: It's not advisable to do your own covers unless you have experience in graphic design.*
*Your cover is your shop window - whether we like it or not people do judge books by their cover.*

# Part 5 - When You Need A Break

### 2. All About You

Write your ABOUT THE AUTHOR, no one likes to write about themselves and let's be honest you're probably going to re-write it hundreds of times - best to get the first draft out of the way. Of course if you decide you don't want to do all these things yourself give us a call and we can support you through you publishing journey.

### 3. About Your Book

Time to write your DUST JACKET DESCRIPTION, again you will probably change this a number of times, but with the information you have produced in Part 1 of this sheet, you shouldn't have very much to do.

### 4. Press Information

Start thinking about how you will PRESS RELEASE your book. Is there a seasonal or special hook, is there something about you that can hook an editor in? What is the book about - in terms of issues etc…

If you're not sure what to put in a press release it is advisable to get a company like ours who do this professionally to help. Excalibur can offer this service within our vanity publishing packages, in our publicity management packages or as a separate single author service.

### 5. Marketing Plan

Another important part of getting your book out there will be how you garner PUBLICITY, why not start taking some notes on how other local and indie authors are doing it and noting what

seems to be working and what's not.

Be careful not to get too excited and tell everyone all about your book before you're ready to cash in - you don't want them getting bored of hearing you banging on about your book before you've even written it. However, similarly, a little well placed curiosity can help when it finally hits the shelves.

## 6. Research

Remember, although you are writing a book, which essentially is a creative project - what you are actually doing is setting yourself up as a an entrepreneur selling your own product. Make sure you do your MARKET RESEARCH, there's no point releasing a book that has no hope of ever being bought or read.

## 7. Get Educated

You can never have enough INFORMATION when it comes to the creative arts and the great thing is there are plenty of people out there willing to share their top tips with you.

Not all of the tips and advice (as with this document) will be relative to your situation, however, reading new ways of doing things or about other author's experiences can help trigger a thought process or creative stream in your head that will be beneficial.

Don't dismiss the author and publisher self-help websites until you've had a look through them.

# Final Word

· · · · · · · · · · · · · · · · · · · · · · · · · ·

*"Even if you are a best-seller you feel insecure because it is all so unpredictable."*

**- Patricia Cornwell -**

# Final Word

When it comes to taking time away from your writing to do other things concerning your book, make sure you are always spending an equal amount of time on both...or more time writing at the beginning. Don't get caught in a trap where you become an expert in the one thing you aren't doing.

We hope that some of the tips in this guide will help you gain more focus or simply help you plan out that novel you've been thinking about.

For many authors there are many ideas being developed at any one time. By following some of the points in this guide you might find that you can release ideas for other books while concentrating on the one you will release first.

The one thing we would always advise people is to not only get the opinions and feedback of others but to always trust your gut instinct when it comes to the content of your book.

Excalibur Press specialise in supporting both new and established authors through the publishing process. Whether you plan to self-publish and release the book yourself or you would like to publish through our imprint, we can help.

Just remember that every book deserves a space on the shelf and no one should ever tell you that your book isn't good enough to be published. Here's the thing, I'm not the greatest writer in the world, I bet you've found a mistake or two in here. But I write for a living, have done for 20 years. As well as that I'm a publicist and the founder of Excalibur Press. I truly believe that if you dare to dream as long as you're prepared to work hard and take action you'll achieve your goal.

Good Luck with the book, please do let us know when you're finished....

## *Tina Calder :)*

# Final Word

"*We believe every book deserves a space on the shelf*"

**- Excalibur Press -**

## About Excalibur Press

Excalibur Press are a young, dynamic company specialising in media and publishing.

As syndicators of news and photos we have clients which include most major publishers and broadcasters in the UK such as Trinity Mirror, News International, Independent Newspapers, Johnston Press Ltd, BBC, Bauer, UTV and more.

In our journalism department we have new and up-and-coming writers as well as reporters with 20-years experience in the UK, Ireland and Northern Ireland markets.

Our publicist has worked with some of the biggest names in entertainment and showbiz over a ten year career in the UK, Ireland and Northern Ireland.

As well as providing media services we are currently rolling out a boutique publishing programme offers Northern Ireland writers (both amateur and professional) a new and unique opportunity to break into the publishing world.

## About Tina Calder

Excalibur Press founder Tina Calder has a wide and varied career than spans two decades.

The award-winning journalist, publicist and author has been specialising in editorial services and syndicated content throughout her career.

Having specialised in lifestyle, features, showbiz and entertainment for 20 years as well as having a keen interest in business, entrepreneurship and online publishing, Tina has carved a niche for herself and her company writing in a broad range of styles for a wide variety of publications and clients.

Survival: The Story of The Defects is Tina's first book, she is currently working on the biography of former SLF member Henry Cluney among others.

Tina is also the creator of Excalibur Press' own magazine www.bamni.co.uk and her most recent venture The Merlin Project, an ideas and learning platform.

# Your Notes

## Excalibur Press

www.ExcaliburPress.co.uk

www.Facebook.com/ExcaliburNews

www.Twitter.com/ExcaliburPress

## The Merlin Project

www.Facebook.com/MerlinProjectIdeas

www.Twitter.com/Merlin_Project

## BAM Magazine

www.BAMni.co.uk

www.Facebook.com/BAMmagNI

## *Thank You !*

**BONUS: You are invited to become part of the Excalibur Press & The Merlin Project Inner Circle on Facebook, to JOIN the group simply go to:**
**www.facebook.com/groups/ExcaliburInnerCircle**

www.ingramcontent.com/pod-product-compliance
Lightning Source LLC
Chambersburg PA
CBHW060840270326

41933CB00002B/150